Behind the Glamour

BEHIND [THE] SCENES
PRO SPORTS CAREERS

By Danielle S. Hammelef

CAPSTONE PRESS
a capstone imprint

Savvy Books are published by Capstone Press,
1710 Roe Crest Drive, North Mankato, Minnesota 56003
www.mycapstone.com

Library of Congress cataloging-in-publication data is available on the Library of Congress website

ISBN: 978-1-5757-4896-0 (hardcover) -- 978-1-5757-4909-7 (eBook PDF)

Summary: Fascinating facts, fun pictures, and easy-to-read sidebars highlight informative text about some of the most interesting jobs that take place behind the scenes in professional sports. Readers will get a glimpse at what it takes to make it as a talent scout, sportscaster, team mascot, and more and find out what goes on behind the glamour.

Editor: Alison Deering
Designer: Heidi Thompson and Kayla Rossow
Media reseacher: Pam Mitsakos
Production specialist: Tori Abraham

Image Credits: Alamy: Action Plus Sports Images, 16 top right, Jim West, 27, ZUMA Press Inc, 33 top left; Getty Images: Christopher Morris, 59, Clive Mason, 41 top left, Fort Worth Star-Telegram, 28 top left, Sarah Crabill, 35 top left; iStockphoto: fotostorm, 16 bottom left, Steve Cole, 11 top right, Steve Debenport, 35 top right, sturti, 12 bottom left; Newscom: ARIC CRABB/TNS, 26 top middle, Elizabeth Flores/ZUMA Press, 52, Gwendoline Le Goff/ZUMAPRESS, 58 bottom right, Hector Acevedo/ZUMA Press, 53, PHIL MASTURZO/ KRT, 47, Stephen M. Dowell/ABACAUSA.COM, 57 middle left; Shutterstock: a katz, 58 top right, Adam Gregor, 16 bottom right, amie cross, 22, ANATOMIA3D, 14 top left, Andrey_Popov, 12 middle left, 24 middle right, 31, Andrii Kobryn, 29 bottom right, antoniodiaz, 21 bottom right, anucha maneechote, 43 bottom left, Ariwasabi, 19 top right, Aspen Photo, 9 middle left, 15 bottom right, 42, 50 bottom left, bikeriderlondon, 5, 30 middle right, 38 middle left, Capifrutta, 38 top right, Corepics VOF, 7 top middle, CP DC Press, 46 top right, Creativa Images, 39 top left, CruZeWizard, 60 top left, Dean Drobot, 30 top right, Dmitri Ma, 30 bottom right, DW labs Incorporated, 6 right, 34 bottom left, 60 top right, Elena Schweitzer, 18, Eric Broder Van Dyke, 34 top right, ESB Professional, 10, EsraKeskinSenay, 6 background, gpointstudio, 37, Gromovataya, 51 top, Igor Bulgarin, 55 middle left, imagestockdesign, 36, Ivica Drusany, 55 top left, Jonah_H, 40 bottom right, Joseph Sohm, 43 top left, 49 middle, Kzenon, 13, 17 bottom left, L.F, 20 bottom right, Lance Bellers, 49 bottom left, lev radin, 26 top left, 56, Lindsay Franklin, 49 top left, Lopolo, 20 top right, Lukasz Libuszewski, 61, Mat Hayward, 48, michaeljung, cover top left, Monkey Business Images, 14 middle right, 38 bottom left, 60 bottom left, muzsy, 7 bottom right, Nata Sha, 57 middle right, Nebojsa Markovic, 44 top left, oksana2010, 38 top middle, pedalist, 4, Photographee.eu, 23, Phovoir, 50 top right, Pressmaster, 40 top left, Production Perig, 9 bottom right, Rasulov, 21 middle right, Richard Paul Kane, 44 bottom left, 46 bottom right, Rommel Canlas, cover right, Sergey Kuznecov, 45 top left, Sergey Novikov, 50 middle left, Tony Bowler, 26 top right, Tumar, 8, Tyler Olson, 17 top left, Undrey, 55 bottom left, VectorLifestylepic, 14 top right, wavebreakmedia, 1, 15 middle right, 24 top right, 25 top, 32, WAYHOME studio, 41 bottom right, Yulia Mayorova, 28 middle right; Thinkstock: Polka Dot Images, 29 top middle

Design Elements: Capstone Studio: Karon Dubke; Shutterstock: helen-light, My Life Graphic, optimarc, winui

Source Credits: p. 10 from www.studentdoctor.net/2013/05/20-questions-c-david-geier-jr-md; p. 47 from www.makers.com/violet-palmer; p. 52 from www.monster.com/career-advice/article/manage-a-sports-facility

Printed in Canada.
010039S17

Table of Contents

INTRODUCTION
Crazy About Sports

If you're reading this, chances are you're crazy about sports. Maybe you love soccer and the thrill of intercepting a pass. Maybe you can't get enough of basketball — the squeak of rubber on polished floors and the swish of the nothing-but-net balls. Or maybe you live for the sweet crack of the bat that sends a baseball sailing over an outfielder's head. Whether you play or just watch sports, you are among millions of people around the world who love athletic competition.

When most people picture their dream jobs in sports, they think about the glamorous lifestyles of professional athletes. You see them at sports stadiums or watch the competitions on television. But these athletes don't build or run their own stadiums. They don't announce play-by-play action. And athletes aren't stitching up their own cuts on the field. Athletes need people working behind the cameras and microphones to help them perform their best. They need talented sports enthusiasts just like you who want to build careers focused on professional sports.

Almost any of your talents can be used to find a job in sports, whether you have a knack for writing or making friends. The career possibilities are endless — from being a team doctor or athletic trainer to finding skilled players for a professional team as a talent scout. Each job needs savvy sports fans like you who want to be part of the game.

CHAPTER 1

Team Physician

Injuries are part of sports. Even athletes who are in top physical condition get hurt. Sports teams rely on one of their most important team members — the team physician — to get their athletes back into the game as soon as possible. This highly educated individual doesn't wear a team uniform. But he or she has trained for 12 to 16 years to be part of a team's staff. If you want to be a doctor and work in sports, you can do both as a team physician.

Professional sports teams each have their own team physician. A glamorous perk of being a professional sports team doctor is that you attend all home games and travel with the team to away games.

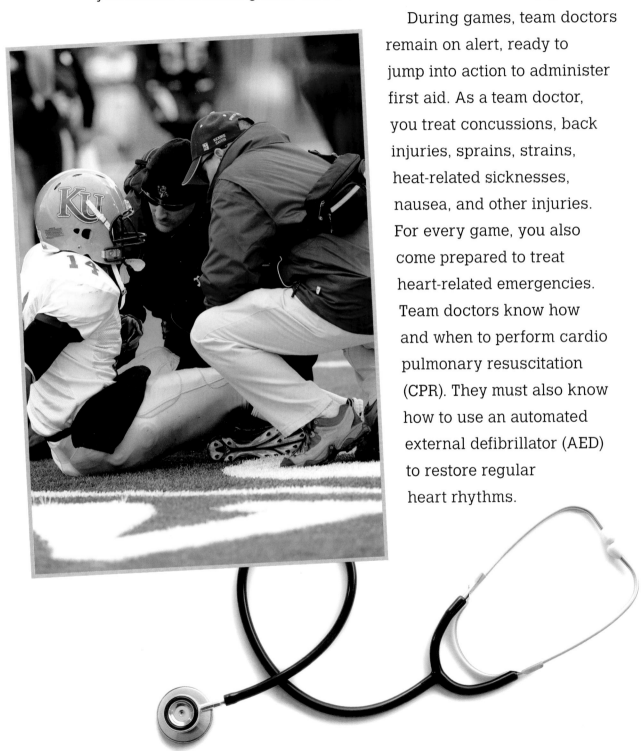

During games, team doctors remain on alert, ready to jump into action to administer first aid. As a team doctor, you treat concussions, back injuries, sprains, strains, heat-related sicknesses, nausea, and other injuries. For every game, you also come prepared to treat heart-related emergencies. Team doctors know how and when to perform cardio pulmonary resuscitation (CPR). They must also know how to use an automated external defibrillator (AED) to restore regular heart rhythms.

MEET DR. C. DAVID GEIER JR., MD, SPORTS MEDICINE

When asked why he wanted to become a doctor, Dr. C. David Geier Jr. said, "I wanted a career that would challenge me every day. I felt like whatever field I ultimately chose within medicine, I would have new problems to solve, new diagnoses to make, and new opportunities to make people better."

Dr. Geier is excited about the future of sports medicine. "I think that sports medicine will continue to advance with new technology and equipment to treat athletes' injuries better surgically. The rehabilitation and medical treatments available will improve as well. I expect that we will be able to get athletes and people who like to exercise to have longer careers and be able to play sports and exercise longer and more successfully than ever before."

If athletes suffer injuries that prevent them from playing, team physicians take charge of coordinating recovery. As a team doctor, it will be your responsibility to explain athletes' medical conditions

and recovery plans. You will need to be able to detail these things to both the athletes and the coaches so they fully understand the extent of the injuries.

At a Glance

Also known as: Team doctor, orthopedic surgeon, sports medicine specialist

Overview: Team physicians treat athletes on the team for injuries and coordinate medical care for injury recovery.

Education: Undergraduate college degree, followed by four years of medical school and four to five years of post-medical school residency, depending on your degree; surgeon requires five additional years of general orthopedics and one year dedicated to sports medicine; physicians and surgeons must pass a license exam in order to practice their specialty.

Special skills: Confident, empathetic, hardworking, self-motivated, excellent communicator

Salary: $25,000–$68,000/year

One of your biggest responsibilities as a team doctor is giving athletes the "green light" to return to play. Sometimes team physicians face pressure from their patients and coaches to put the athletes back into the game before they're ready. But even though pulling a star player may hurt the team's performance, the long-term health of the athletes should be your focus. A good physician knows putting athletes back in the game before they've fully recovered can lead to worse injuries.

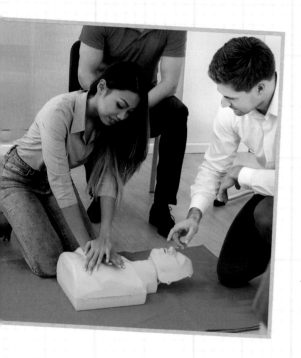

GET AHEAD OF THE GAME

If you think you may have a future in sports medicine, there are things you can do right now to give yourself a head start on this career path.

· Ask your own doctor about his or her job.

· Read and learn as much as you can about the human body.

· Take CPR classes. CPR is a lifesaving technique useful in many emergencies including heart attack or near drowning, in which someone's breathing or heartbeat has stopped.

· Learn how to use an AED. An AED is a portable device that checks the heart rhythm and can send an electric shock to the heart to try to restore a normal rhythm. AEDs are used to treat sudden cardiac arrest (SCA). SCA is a condition in which the heart suddenly and unexpectedly stops beating.

CHAPTER 2

Athletic Trainer

If you like the idea of being a team physican, but not attending 8 to 12 years of school, consider a job as an athletic trainer. Athletic trainers, or ATs, are medical professionals licensed to oversee the daily medical care of athletes. ATs work closely with team doctors.

Your first goal as an AT is injury prevention. Athletic trainers know the names of all 650 muscles in the human body and how muscles work together with ligaments, tendons, and bones. They study what happens to these body parts when injuries occur. As a team athletic trainer, you teach athletes how to exercise and train with proper methods to prevent harm to their bodies.

At a Glance

Also known as: AT, wellness manager, rehabilitation specialist, physician extender

Overview: Athletic trainers oversee the daily medical care of athletes; they prevent and evaluate injuries, give emergency medical treatment, and develop and implement rehabilitation programs.

Education: Bachelor's or master's of science in sports-related areas such as exercise physiology, nutrition, injury prevention, physical rehabilitation, and strength and conditioning; certification exam required

Special skills: Good people skills, excellent communication skills, good listener, creative problem solving, cool under pressure

Salary: $28,000–$69,000/year

HAMSTRING REHABILITATION

Some of the most common muscle injuries are hamstring strains. Hamstrings are a group of three muscles found in the back of the thighs. They stretch between the knee and the hip. How long an athlete needs to recover from a hamstring injury will depend on how severely the muscles were torn. The first step in rehabilitation is immediate implementation of R.I.C.E., which stands for:

- **R**est the injury and protect it from additional harm using slings, crutches, and sitting or lying down.
- **I**ce the area to reduce swelling using ice wrapped in a damp towel for 20 minutes every three to four hours.
- **C**ompression to stabilize and support the injured muscle using compression bandages. Make sure not to wrap these bandages so tightly that they cause numbness.
- **E**levation to lower the blood flow and reduce other fluids from pooling in the area.

R.I.C.E. should be performed for three to five days after an injury. Do not use heat.

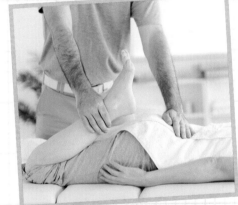

The second step is to regain strength and flexibility in the hamstrings with exercise such as this one:

- Hamstring static flexion: Lie face down and try to bring your heel toward your bottom. Build up to 20 repetitions and repeat five times.

When all of these reps can be done without pain, the next step is performing stretches such as this one:

- Lying down hamstring stretch: Lie on your back and extend your leg toward your chest until you feel a tug in the hamstring. Each time, try to do this with a straight leg.

When athletes get hurt, trainers spring into action. Not all injuries sideline athletes or require doctors' visits. A trainer may only have a time-out to tell if an athlete can get back into the game. Sometimes all the athlete needs is stretches or ice packs. ATs also apply athletic tape, bandages, or wrist, elbow, knee, or ankle braces to athletes before practices and games to protect injuries.

GET AHEAD OF THE GAME

• Learn basic first aid, CPR, and AED.

• Volunteer to help your school's athletic trainer.

• Read up on sports injuries and prevention and treatment.

Athletic trainers also work with team physicians to design custom rehab plans for athletes. Athletes will rely on your knowledge as an AT to explain both their injury diagnoses and rehab programs in clear, easy-to-understand terms.

Like the team physicians and coaches they report to, ATs must know how to make athletes feel comfortable talking to them. Since ATs attend everyday practices as well as games, you'll have the chance to get to know your athletes. The strong personal relationships you and your athletes form will also help them trust that you know what is best for their recovery.

CHAPTER 3

Nutritionist

Food fuels our bodies. But not all foods are created equal. They don't all supply the same amount of energy or basic nutrients. Take the time to compare the nutrition labels on different foods in your cupboard and you might be surprised by what you see — wide-ranging values for calories, fats, proteins, and more.

Just like you, athletes need to eat the right amount of healthy foods in order to maintain, gain, or lose weight, as well as build muscles. If you love staying healthy and active and want to help athletes be the best they can be, check out what it takes to become a sports nutritionist.

At a Glance

Also known as: Sports nutrition counselor

Overview: Nutritionists evaluate the nutritional needs of individual athletes, plan nutritious and healthy meals, and advise athletes on nutritional problems.

Education: Bachelor's degree in sports nutrition or nutrition; pass examination to become licensed as a registered dietician

Special skills: Thorough knowledge of nutrition, good people skills, compassionate, understanding, excellent communication skills, understanding of exercise and fitness

Salary: $35,000–$80,000/year

As a nutritionist, you plan healthy and nutritious meals and menus. Athletes may seek your knowledge because they lack energy or stamina. The right foods can help athletes swim faster, throw harder, or jump higher. You adjust athletes' nutritional needs as they recover from broken bones or pulled muscles so they can get back into the game as quickly as possible. And sometimes your nutritional expertise helps athletes prepare for or recover from intense competitions, such as marathons.

GET AHEAD OF THE GAME

- Read nutrition labels.
- Learn healthy recipes and foods for you and your family.
- Go grocery shopping with your parents or caregiver.
- Stay active and get plenty of rest; be a healthy example to your family and friends.

WHAT'S ON THE MENU?

Athletes perform better if they eat the right foods at the right times to fuel their bodies.

Here's an example of a pregame meal plan.

Dinner Menu — eat the night before the game

Baked salmon

Long-grain rice

Baked potato

Low-fat milk

Strawberries for dessert

Breakfast Menu

Fruit of choice

Skim or low-fat milk

Greek yogurt

Oatmeal

Pregame Lunch Menu — eat three to four hours before the game

Grilled skinless chicken or turkey breast

Whole-grain pasta

Steamed vegetables

Water

Recovery Meal Menu — eat within 30 minutes of the game ending

Chocolate milk

Banana

Nutritionists study foods and know what roles certain foods fulfill for athletes. Foods can be broken down into three major categories: carbohydrates, proteins, and fats.

DIGESTING NUTRITION LABELS

Nutrition facts panels on food packages tell you about the food inside.

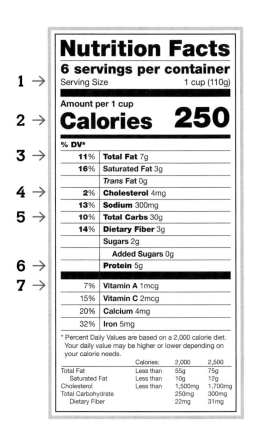

1. **Serving size:** This tells you the size of a single serving and total servings in the package.

2. **Calories per serving:** If you eat double the serving size, you'll double the calories too. This section also tells you how many calories from fat you'll eat in one serving.

3. **Total fat** (broken down into trans fats, saturated fats, polyunsaturated, and monounsaturated fats): Trans fats and saturated fats are unhealthy fats. Look for foods with 0 percent of these fats. Unsaturated fats help your body protect its organs and absorb vitamins.

4. **Cholesterol and sodium:** Look for foods with low percentages to reduce your risks of heart disease and high blood pressure.

5. **Total carbohydrate** (comes from dietary fiber and sugars): Avoid foods with added sugars listed in the ingredients as sucrose, glucose, fructose, or corn or maple syrup. These add calories but not vitamins and minerals to foods. Look for natural sources of carbs instead.

6. **Protein:** Necessary for healthy skin, blood, hair, and muscle building and repair. Choose lean, low-fat, or fat-free sources such as skim milk, fish, and beans.

7. **Vitamins and minerals:** Look for high amounts of these as compared to the number of calories to help you select healthier foods.

CHAPTER 4

Psychologist

As someone who loves sports, you know that the best athletes are both physically and mentally strong. Muhammad Ali, World Heavyweight Champion boxer, once said, "Champions aren't made in the gyms. Champions are made from something they have deep inside them — a desire, a dream, a vision." Athletes train their bodies with drills and healthy diets, but sometimes they need help overcoming performance stress or frustration while recovering from injuries. If you want to help athletes get back to the top of their mental game, then sports psychology may be a career for you.

When the doubts and negative thoughts such as "What if I mess up?" creep into athletes' minds, sports psychologists teach their patients how to think positively instead. In confidential discussions, psychologists help athletes become aware of their negative self-talk. Then they teach them mental tricks to change the negative talk into positive thoughts.

For example, sports psychologists teach their patients to use mental stop signs. In this brain trick, athletes tell themselves "Stop!" whenever negative thoughts start. They may even picture a stop sign or a red light in their minds. Then they replace the negative thought with a phrase such as, "I've got this."

GET AHEAD OF THE GAME

- Learn as much as you can about different sports and play sports so you can understand the pressures athletes face to perform, as well as to recover from injuries.
- Take psychology classes in high school.

Some athletes need positive thinking skills to handle performance anxiety. Sports psychologists teach athletes to build upon positive self-talk with visual imagery. They teach patients to see themselves successfully performing their tasks moment-by-moment and step-by-step. This visualization brain training sends messages to athletes' muscles to make memories of how to move.

So when the athletes actually perform, their muscles already know what to do to jump higher or run faster. Injured athletes often learn visualization so they can keep training without physical workouts.

At a Glance

Also known as: Sport and exercise psychologist

Overview: A sports psychologist helps athletes prepare for competition and deal with pressures of performing.

Education: Bachelor's degree in sports science or psychology, master's or doctorate degree in sports psychology, sports psychology internships, state licensing exam

Special skills: Love of sports, understanding of athletic pressures, empathetic, good listener, desire to help others

Salary: $40,000–$118,000/year

SUPERSTITIOUS PRO-ATHLETES

Sports are filled with athletes who perform certain routines before every game or keep "lucky" items. Here are some of the strangest superstitions in pro-sports:

- Michael Jordan wore his University of North Carolina basketball shorts underneath his Chicago Bulls uniform.
- Wade Boggs ate chicken before every baseball game.
- Tiger Woods always wears a red shirt on the final day of golf tournament play.
- National Hockey League players never shave their beards during the playoffs.
- Larry Walker always took three practice swings before coming up to bat.
- Brian Urlacher always ate two chocolate chip cookies before every football game.
- Steve Kline never washed his sweaty baseball cap all season.
- Jason Terry slept in the shorts of his next basketball opponent the nights leading up to the game.
- Hockey goalie Patrick Roy always talked to the goalposts behind him.
- Serena Williams wears the same pair of socks throughout each tournament.
- Turk Wendall always ate four pieces of black licorice during the games he pitched.
- Mike Bibby clipped his fingernails during every time-out during the basketball game.
- British diver Tom Daley keeps a lucky stuffed orange monkey.

CHAPTER 5
Talent Scout

Have you ever stopped to wonder how pro-sports teams find their players? After all, you can't just show up and walk onto the field or court. Teams rely on sports scouts to evaluate athletes' talents and personalities. If you love to attend sporting events and have sharp observation skills, then scouting may be the career for you.

Professional scouts spend lots of time traveling to and watching sporting events to study athletes in action. General managers, coaches, and team owners count on scouts to be their "eyes in the field" to find players who are right for their teams.

At a Glance

Also known as: Scout

Overview: Talent scouts find and evaluate athletes for sports teams.

Education: Bachelor's degree in sports management or sports administration; coaching experience helpful

Special skills: Keen observer of talent, personality, and character; excellent communication skills; persuasive; sincere and believable

Salary: $18,000–$70,000/year

If you've ever seen someone at a track and field meet with a stopwatch and clipboard handing out business cards to coaches, then you've probably seen a scout. You also find scouts holding radar guns near home plate measuring how fast a pitcher throws. As a scout, you watch players perform many times before deciding if they have the skills to compete on a professional level. Scouts also watch recorded competition highlights and read player stats in the news.

GET AHEAD OF THE GAME

· Read the sports section of newspapers.
· Talk to your local high school or college coaches about when scouts would attend games and try to arrange a meeting to ask them about their job.
· Talk to coaches about what kind of information they seek when scouting a player or team.
· Observe athletes and note how well they perform at their sports as well as their attitudes on and off the field.

But an athlete's numbers don't always tell the whole story. Scouts understand that athletes' personalities also play a large role in a team's success. Not only is a good scout an excellent judge of talent but also an excellent judge of character.

Scouts watch athletes during practices and note how they act toward their teammates and coaches. In scouting reports, they record how players respond to coaching instructions. Coaches want players who are willing to work hard, even when faced with defeat.

Not all scouts are out to find new talent, though. Some professional scouts analyze how other teams play the game to help give their own team insight on how to beat their opponents. They watch live games and study video footage to look for the other team's strengths and weaknesses.

TALK LIKE A BASEBALL SCOUT

Baseball scouts have their own slang terms for their scouting reports. Here are just a few:

- All-American out = a poor hitter
- All-or-nothing = power hitter who usually strikes out if he or she doesn't hit a home run
- Bad paws = a player who has trouble holding onto the ball
- Bat breaker = a hard hitter whose powerful swings often break the bat
- Burner = a very fast base runner
- Base clogger = slow runner
- Can't miss = said of a young player who appears to be headed for baseball success
- DNF = short for draft and follow; said of a high school or junior college player who was drafted, but doesn't have a signed contract yet
- Fireplug = a short, stocky player
- KP = short for can't play; player with no future in baseball
- NP = short for no prospect = player who will not reach the major leagues
- Plowhorse = player who keeps performing well even after others think he or she would have let up
- Soft tosser = pitcher who throws off-speed pitches
- Surveyor = a player with a good eye at the plate and who gets lots of walks because he or she only swings at balls in the strike zone
- Workhorse = tireless pitcher who plays in many games or a large number of innings during the season

CHAPTER 6

Sportscaster

When they can't make it to the game, millions of sports fans tune into their televisions and radios to watch and listen to sporting events. Fans rely on sportscasters to give them play-by-play descriptions of the action taking place. If you live for talking about sports, you could one day be one of the men and women behind the microphones.

Sportscasters live, eat, and sleep sports. They stay up-to-date on the world of sports and do their homework before every broadcast. Their pre-game studies give them facts and stories to toss in during breaks in the action to keep fans interested. As a sportscaster, your own enthusiasm for sports shines through when you comment on the players, coaches, game officials, and live action.

At a Glance

Also known as: Sports reporter, sports announcer

Overview: Sportscasters report sports news to television and/or radio audiences.

Education: Bachelor's degree in communications, broadcasting, television production, or journalism; minor degree in sports administration or physical education is helpful

Special skills: Clear and pleasant speaking voice, writing skills, communication skills, knowledge of sports, easygoing personality, ability to ad-lib

Salary: $29,000–$122,000/year

Fans of both teams tune in to the broadcasts, so as a sportscaster, your comments give fair air time to each team. Sportscasters often work in teams. One commentator will tell the fans what's going on in the game. The other may be on the field interviewing coaches, players, and fans during time-outs and before and after the game.

GET AHEAD OF THE GAME

- If your school has a daily or weekly news announcement crew, get as much airtime as you can. Even working the cameras and mics is valuable experience.
- If your student news broadcast, newspaper, or blog doesn't have a sports feature, volunteer as the school's sports reporter and inspire everyone with your enthusiasm for sports.
- Start a sports blog for your team or your own personal sports blog.
- Practice your interviewing and writing skills.
- Watch and listen to as many sportscasters as you can. If you love sharing your excitement for sports, you've probably practiced announcing games and races right in your own home, maybe even your own play-by-play as you dribble, fake, and swish the championship-winning shot.

SPORTSCASTER KRISTA VODA AT A NASCAR EVENT

The best sportscasters entertain, inform, and educate the viewers all at the same time. Sportscasters bring the action to life with colorful and dramatic vocabulary. Listeners want to hear announcers' excitement when a team scores. They want to feel the frustration when a game official makes a poor call or a player loses control of the ball or puck.

If sportscasters show that they know the rules and strategies, language of the game, and history of the players, fans will trust what they say. Sportscasters explain what's happening in such a way that die-hard fans understand and casual listeners won't get lost. Fast game action doesn't allow time to look up player stats. Instead, sportscasters rely on excellent memories to recall trivia about players and previous seasons.

INTERVIEW LIKE A PRO

Whether you're interviewing a
famous sports star or a crazy fan,
the best interviews take planning
and communication savvy.
Here are 10 tips:

1. Set goals. Outline what you want to
   discuss and what information you
   want from the person you're interviewing.

2. Study. Find out as much as you can about the person so you can ask questions that no one
   else has ever asked him or her before.

3. Prepare your guest. Let him or her know how much time you'll need, who your audience is,
   and what types of questions you want to ask.

4. Choose a location. Ask your guest where he or she would feel most comfortable being interviewed.

5. Break the ice. Your first question should always be something to get the conversation started.
   Ask questions such as, "Where did you grow up?" and "Why did you choose your career?"

6. Listen. A good interview is a two-way conversation. Let your guest finish answering every
   question, and never interrupt with your own opinions and ideas.

7. Keep questions open-ended. Never ask questions that only need a "yes" or "no" answer.
   Instead, ask "when" and "how" and "why" questions that require explanations.

8. Take a breath. After your guest answers your question, wait before asking the next question
   to see if he or she will add more.

9. Ask a question that's not related to the topic. Get insight into your guest's personality by asking
   questions such as, "What did you want to be when you grew up?" or "Who is your hero?"

10. Have fun. Stay relaxed and enjoy the person's company. Your guest will feel relaxed and
    match your mood.

CHAPTER 7
Statistician

Anyone who watches live sporting events on television or listens to them on the radio has seen or heard the work of sports statisticians. Sports broadcasters use player and team statistics or "stats" while commenting on a game or interviewing players and coaches. If you love both sports and math, becoming a sports statistician lets you combine your favorite interests into an exciting number-crunching career.

Statistics start with collecting data. The biggest perk of being a sports statistician is watching every moment of a sporting event to collect your data. You record details about how many times something happened and who did what.

GET AHEAD OF THE GAME

- Volunteer to record stats for your team, your school's team, etc.
- Volunteer as scorekeeper.
- Take computer classes to learn spread sheets.
- Read histories of sports and learn all rules and terminology.
- Talk with coaches and find out what kind of information they would need or find helpful to improve their team.

Statisticians are computer savvy and keep track of this information on spreadsheets. As the game continues, they use their analytical skills.

Sports analysts look at their figures and decide if a player or team is performing as expected, better, or worse. They send the updated numbers to announcers to use in live commentaries. As a sports analyst, you help create visual pictures of team and player facts using tables, graphs, and charts for TV audiences.

At a Glance

Also known as: Sports statistical analyst
Overview: A sports statistician collects, analyzes, and interprets sports data.
Education: Computer-programming classes, bachelor's degree in mathematics, master's degree in statistics
Special skills: Computer skills, math skills, thorough knowledge of sports, logical, ability to explain complicated math in easy-to-understand ways
Salary: $39,000–$119,000/year

Your work as a statistician reaches beyond immediate broadcasts too. Sports writers will quote your stats in their daily articles printed about games. Fans read your player stats printed in game programs or published in team books. Leagues use your statistical data for their official record books.

Teams use the statistician's work to decide a player's value to the team. Players who perform well according to their stats may be given bigger contracts. Teams also use stats to make decisions about their starting players to increase their chances of winning.

Sometimes, stats tell teams it's time to cut or trade a player whose performance shows a downward trend. And if teams decide to change their lineup, their scouts rely on sports analysts' numbers to find new athletes. Scouts read player performance trends based on your analyses.

CRUNCH NUMBERS LIKE A PRO

You can calculate some of the most common sports stats using the math formulas behind baseball, basketball, hockey, and soccer stats.

- How to calculate batting average:
Hits/At Bats = Batting Average

- How to calculate field goal percentage (FG%) in basketball:
FG% = number of baskets made/ total number of shots tried

- How to calculate save percentage for hockey, soccer, and other sports' goalies:
Save percentage = saves/shots against goal

CHAPTER 8

Game Official

Every sport has its own set of rules. And every sport needs experts who have memorized every rule to oversee the competitions and make sure everyone plays fairly. These experts are the umpires, referees, linesmen, scorekeepers, and goal judges. If you like being in charge and playing by the rules, then read on about this game-changing career.

Although every sport's rules are different, the basic job of the officials is the same. It's their job to ensure fair play. As the sports official, you keep all the information from those thick rule books in your head. Unless your sport has instant-replay cameras for reviewing plays, once you make a call, your decision stands.

GET AHEAD OF THE GAME

- Volunteer to be a line judge at youth volleyball games.
- Watch umpires and referees in action to learn how they make their calls.
- Read and memorize the rule books of the sports you want to officiate.
- Most refs and umps love to talk to someone who politely asks questions about their job and training (as opposed to being yelled at or booed during game play) so talk to as many as you can. This may also lead you to real on-the-job experience. Sometimes it's who you know that helps you land that job.

With the exception of baseball umpires, most game officials wear their key piece of officiating equipment — their whistles — around their necks. Whenever officials see a player breaking the rules, they blow their whistles to stop play. And once play is stopped, it's your job as the official to explain to players, coaches, and fans why you blew your whistle. Officials give penalties for actions such as unnecessary contact with another player, illegal use of their hands or equipment, or being in the wrong position at the time of play.

As an official, you also stop play for out-of-bounds, off-sides, time-outs, and injuries to players. Baseball umpires decide if runners are safe or out. Behind home plate, umpires watch every pitch and decide if it is a strike or ball. Soccer, lacrosse, and hockey goal judges decide if goals are scored. Track and swimming officials make sure every athlete starts at the same time and no one jumps the gun.

Officials need to clearly see and judge the action at all times. They try to position themselves on the field to avoid interfering with the action. Of course, staying out of the way of a charging athlete also keeps you off the injury list!

Since officials need to be in the right place at the right time to make fair calls, they need to be in excellent physical shape. Hockey referees and linesmen skate up and down the ice all game along with the players, hustling from end to end on fast breaks on goal. Soccer, basketball, and football officials run alongside the players watching for penalties.

At a Glance

Also known as: Referee, umpire, line judge
Overview: Game officials enforce game rules and decide game arguments.
Education: Certification is required to officiate at the college and pro levels of play.
Special skills: Physically fit, self-confident, excellent and quick judgment, knowledge of rules of the game, handle stress well
Salary: Dependent on the sport — NFL: $2,500–$3,000/game; NHL: $1,400–$2,700/game; MLB umpire salaries are not public, however they are estimated to be $120,000–$350,000/year.

Another of the officials' responsibilities is using correct signals. Officials learn hand, arm, and even leg signals that are unique to each sport. If you're a soccer referee, you signal a goal kick by pointing a straight arm toward the goal with your palm open. Football officials signal tripping penalties by sweeping their right feet behind their left heels.

Most importantly, it is critical that officials control their emotions. Referees must make quick, fair, and consistent decisions. However, for any call you make as a referee, one side won't be happy. When officials call penalties, players, coaches, and even fans may argue the referees' decisions. Fans may boo or call officials names. Coaches and players may get in their faces or even throw things out of frustration. As a referee, you must remain calm, cool, and collected while others question your judgment.

MEET VIOLET PALMER,
THE FIRST FEMALE NBA REFEREE

On October 31, 1997, after working as a professional referee for college basketball, Violet Palmer made sports history and became the first woman NBA referee. Palmer remembers hearing whispers of, "Oh my god, the woman is here," the first time she stepped on the court. "I was scared out of my wits," she said, "because I just knew the world was waiting for me to fall on my face."

In 2006, Palmer became the first woman ref to be asked to officiate an NBA playoff game. The NBA only selects a handful of its refs to officiate high-pressure postseason games where every game can mean players' and coaches' jobs are on the line.

> OF HER ACCOMPLISHMENTS PALMER SAID,
> "I'M GIVEN THE RESPECT AS A WOMAN,
> BUT I'VE EARNED THE RESPECT AS A REFEREE."

CHAPTER 9
Facility Manager

Imagine attending an NFL game to cheer on your favorite football team. With your ticket stub in hand, you weave through the packed crowds, buy some pizza and a drink, and find your section. You squeeze in front of already-seated fans in your litter-free row. Before unfolding your seat, you spot your favorite player warming up on the field with sprints. The arena clock counts down until game time: 3:30, 3:29, 3:28 . . .

Spectators at games want to enjoy themselves without worrying about safety issues such as broken seats or crumbling stairs. They don't want to use dirty, smelly bathrooms, or go hungry or thirsty because food vendors run out of snacks or beverages. And they don't want the game to be delayed because the grounds crew isn't done working.

The people who make events run smoothly are the sports facility managers. If you think being in charge of where your team plays — the money, the security, and the people who work there — sounds interesting, then sports facility management may be for you. Managing a sports venue is like planning and throwing huge parties for thousands of guests and making sure everyone has safe and clean fun.

As an athletic facilities manager, you oversee the day-to-day operations of football fields, basketball arenas, baseball stadiums, tennis courts, ice rinks, swimming pools, golf courses, or other playing surfaces. You oversee employees who write and edit marketing materials to promote special fan giveaways and sales. You're also in charge of departments that hire vendors to sell team hats and shirts as well as food and beverages for game-day concessions.

GET AHEAD OF THE GAME

- Try organizing your own fun race with friends.
- Organize a baseball, soccer, or other sports tournament with your friends.
- Talk to the Zamboni driver at a local hockey rink about caring for the ice surface.
- Interview local groundskeepers about the impact of weather on their playing fields.
- Volunteer to help set up or take down nets, etc., at school or local tournaments.
- Manage a school club, including the financial responsibilities.

For avid sports fans, the biggest perk of becoming a sports-facility director is meeting coaches, athletes, team owners, and fans. And although you attend every home game, you won't have time to sit and cheer along with the spectators. When the fun starts for fans, managers kick into high gear to keep the fun going. While sirens blare and lights flash to celebrate a home team score, they may be calling janitors to mop up a spill. As a director, you must keep cool under pressure and think fast to solve problems. When issues occur and fans don't even realize it, you know you've done your job well.

At a Glance

Also known as: Venue manager; arena director; director of facility operations; stadium manager; stadium director; athletic facilities manager

Overview: A facility manager oversees activities and operations of sports venues and supervises staff.

Education: Bachelor's degree in sports administration, finance, business, recreation management, or marketing

Special skills: Sales abilities, business skills, communication skills, multitasking ability, detail-orientated, managerial skills, organized

Salary: $26,000–$90,000/year

IN THE TRENCHES WITH PETE CARLSON

Pete Carlson is the director of ice arena operations and programming for the National Sports Center Super Rink in Blaine, Minnesota. He earned a bachelor's degree in physical education to start his operations management career. His job responsibilities include overseeing five managers who themselves supervise anywhere from 10 to 15 employees. Most days, Carlson manages schedules and budgeting, deals with mechanical issues and expenses, and looks for ways to attract business.

" A GOOD MANAGER HAS WORKED THE TRENCHES," SAYS CARLSON. "THEY'VE BEEN THE GUY SCRUBBING FLOORS. THEY'VE BEEN THE PERSON ANSWERING PHONE CALLS, THEY'VE BEEN IN MEETINGS WITH FACILITY DIRECTORS. ON-THE-JOB TRAINING IS HOW A LOT OF US LEARNED. "

CHAPTER 10

Team Mascot

The Milwaukee Brewers have their Famous Racing Sausages. The Denver Nuggets have Rocky the Mountain Lion. The Chicago Bulls have Benny the Bull. Most professional sports teams have a mascot to be the fun, energetic face of the team all year long. While playing dress up, mascots act silly in front of huge crowds. If you've ever wanted to take the field as a team's larger-than-life cheerleader, then take a look at the career underneath the colorful costumes.

Underneath fur or feathers, mascots don't worry about personal embarrassment — no one will recognize you. In fact, sports fans expect mascots to be comedians and make every game fun to watch, even if their team is losing. As the person inside the suit, you bring the character to life for fans.

But not just anyone can be a professional mascot. Like casting calls for movies, professional teams hold auditions for team mascots. You can prepare for auditions by attending a mascot training school.

At a Glance

Also known as: Sports mascot
Overview: A mascot entertains fans at sporting events.
Education: College degree and experience as team mascot, training at mascot school
Special skills: Athletic, creative, acting experience, ability to mime
Salary: $25,000–$100,000+ per year

Mascot schools teach how to bring characters to life as lovable, entertaining, and memorable team representatives. Although mascots are comic cheerleaders, they never speak. Training schools teach mascots to be masters at miming and gesturing so their body language speaks louder than spoken words. Mascots pretend to fight, be hurt, and show anger, embarrassment, or laughter.

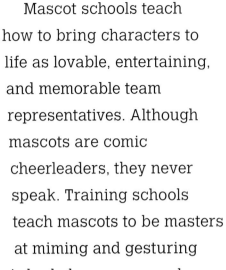

GET AHEAD OF THE GAME

- Gain acting experience in school or community theater productions.
- Study working team mascots to find out how they entertain the fans.
- Volunteer as a school mascot or a parade character.
- Take acting classes, especially how to improvise.
- Stay fit by participating in sports, exercising, and eating healthy foods.

MASCOT MATCH-UP

Mascots from professional football, soccer, baseball, hockey, and basketball teams are listed below. See how many you recognize!

MASCOT	PROFESSIONAL TEAM
Wally the Green Monster	Boston Red Sox
Paws	Detroit Tigers
Raymond	Tampa Bay Rays
Screech	Washington Nationals
Southpaw	Chicago White Sox
Howler	Arizona Coyotes
Blades	Boston Bruins
Stormy	Carolina Hurricanes
Tommy Hawk	Chicago Blackhawks
Youpii!	Montreal Canadiens
Iceburgh	Pittsburgh Penguins
Spartacat	Ottawa Senators

MLB TEAM MASCOTS

MASCOT	PROFESSIONAL TEAM
Moose	Winnipeg Jets
Go the Gorilla	Phoenix Suns
Lucky the Leprechaun	Boston Celtics

FRED THE RED

Stuff the Magic Dragon	Orlando Magic
Gunnersaurus Rex	Arsenal
Captain Canary	Norwich
Fred the Red	Manchester United
Edgar, Allan, and Poe	Baltimore Ravens
Roary	Detroit Lions
Toro the Bull	Houston Texans
Swoop	Philadelphia Eagles
Captain Fear	Tampa Bay Buccaneers
Sourdough Sam	San Francisco 49ers

At mascot school, you learn how to choreograph routines as well as improvise. You learn how to read and respond to crowds, how to deal with the press, and what to do if you accidentally frighten a fan. Your classes teach you tips and tricks for engaging fans and making them laugh, as well as how to motivate fans when their team is losing.

As a team mascot, one minute you'll leap from a trampoline to slam dunk a basketball, and the next you'll hug a young fan and pose for a photo. The more unpredictable and creative mascots are, the more they get the fans into the game. Whether you're jumping through hoops, dancing on dugouts, or sliding across courts on your belly, you become a fan favorite because crowds never know what you'll do next.

CHAPTER 11

Stay in the Game

From sailing to soccer, athletes from around the world compete to be the best they can be. And millions of sports fans attend live competitions or tune in every day to watch or listen to the action remotely. Athletes need talented people to keep them on their toes. Fans need people to help make their sporting experiences exciting.

Maybe you'll choose a career helping athletes prevent and recover from injuries. Maybe you'll sit behind a microphone, losing your voice after announcing the soccer World Cup Championship game. Or maybe you'll be the math whiz computing game stats for the big leagues. Whatever talents you have, hundreds of sports careers await savvy sports fans like you who want to stay in the game.

READ MORE

Cohn, Jessica. *On the Job in the Game*. Concord, Mass.: Red Chair Press, 2016.

Johnson, Jeremy. *Unusual and Awesome Jobs in Sports*. You Get Paid for THAT? North Mankato, Minn.: Capstone Press, 2015.

Raymos, Rick. *STEM Jobs in Sports*. STEM Jobs You'll Love. Vero Beach, Fla: Rourke Educational Media, 2014.

Wunderlich, Richard. *Math on the Job: Working in Sports*. New York: Crabtree Publishing Company, 2016.

INTERNET SITES

FactHound offers a fun, safe way to find Internet sites related to this book. All the sites on FactHound have been researched by our staff.

Here's all you do:

Visit www.facthound.com

Type in this code: 9781515748960

ABOUT THE AUTHOR

Danielle S. Hammelef is the author of more than 17 books for children, including the Capstone Blazer Special Effects series on movies. She has also written award-winning children's magazine stories, nonfiction articles, poetry, and puzzles. Danielle loves to watch animated films and has lost track of how many times she's seen her favorites such as *The Incredibles*, *Shrek*, and *Finding Nemo*. Before becoming a freelance writer, Danielle earned a degree in environmental engineering from Michigan Technological University. Danielle currently lives in Novi, Michigan, with her family.

WANT TO LEARN MORE ABOUT
THE CAREERS BEHIND THE SCENES
IN SOME OF THE WORLD'S MOST
GLAMOROUS INDUSTRIES?

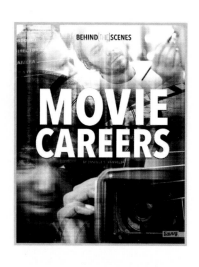  

CHECK OUT THESE TITLES TO GO
Behind the Glamour
IN MOVIES, MUSIC, AND FASHION.